The Jesse Tree - An Advent

As Christians, we look to the Old Testament prophets, kings, and judges to point the way to the Messiah. We also look to the descendants of Abraham from whom the Messiah would come. The Jesse Tree uses symbols (ornaments) of biblical characters from both the Old and New Testaments, to help us "prepare the way of the Lord."

There are three components to a Jesse Tree - the tree, the scriptures and the symbols. The Jesse Tree can be done in different ways, depending on how you and your family prefer to celebrate advent. The tree itself may be a simple potted branch, a small Christmas tree, a banner or poster hung on a wall; be creative. The symbols may be made by you and your family, you can purchase a set of ornaments or you can find objects around the house.

There are 28 days in the longest Advent. This book is a companion to the Jesse Tree Treasures Painted ornament set and it contains 28 scripture stories and symbols.

Many people prefer to follow the scriptures chronologically. We do it randomly, because then during a short advent we can hear the later stories as well as some earlier ones. We hang one ornament on the tree, read the story and sing a song that is appropriate for Advent. Most Advents, you will not use all of your ornaments. Either leave the extra ornaments off or on Christmas Eve add all the remaining ornaments and pick one story (or more if you like). On Christmas Day we place the last ornament on the tree we sing a Christmas Carroll like "O Come Let Us Adore Him."

Have fun, be creative and make the Jesse Tree a unique Advent tradition for your family.

The Earth - Creation
(Genesis 1:1-2:4)

In the beginning God created the heavens and the earth. God said "Let there be light!" The light he called day and the darkness he called night. And so there was the first day. On the second day, God created the sky. When the third day came God made the land and the sea. He filled the land with all kinds of plants. The fourth day, God made two great lights; the sun to rule the day and the moon to rule the night. On the fifth day, God created the birds of the air, the fish in the sea and the animals on the earth. On the sixth day God spoke and made human beings. He breathed his breath of life into them. On the seventh day God looked at his creation. He saw that it was good. He blessed the seventh day and rested from his work.

The Apple - Adam and Eve
(Genesis 3:1-24)

Adam and Eve lived in a beautiful garden called Eden. God said "You may not eat the fruit on the tree that gives knowledge of good and evil." The snake saw Eve in the garden near that tree. He said "Go ahead and eat the apple from that tree." Eve said "Oh no. God said we could not eat the fruit on that tree or we will die." The evil snake said, "You would not die. If you eat the apple you will become like God. It's OK. Eat it." So, Eve ate the apple. Then she gave the apple to Adam and he ate it also. Suddenly, they were filled with knowledge. They heard God coming, so they hid. But God found them and asked "Why are you hiding from me." They answered "Because we are naked." God said "Who told you that you were naked? Have you eaten from the tree of knowledge?" Adam said "Eve gave me the apple." Eve said "The snake tricked me." God was sad because they had not obeyed.

The Ark - Noah
(Genesis 6:9-9:17)

The people God created had become evil. Noah loved God. He was not evil. God spoke to Noah and said, "I am going to send a great flood that will destroy all the evil, everything on earth will die. Build an ark and fill it with two of every creature on earth. Take your wife and your children with you on the ark." Noah obeyed God. The rains came. It rained for forty days and forty nights. When the rains had stopped, Noah sent out a dove. Seven days later it returned with a fresh olive branch. So, Noah knew the water was going down. When all the waters were gone Noah and his family and all the animals came out of the ark. God promised never to send a flood to wipe out everything on the earth again. Then, God placed a rainbow in the sky as a sign of His promise.

The Camel - Abraham
(Genesis 15:1-21)

Abraham was a man who loved God very much. He was a nomad, a wandering herder with no land to call his own. One day, God spoke to Abraham and said, "You will have as many descendants as there are stars in the sky." Although he had no children and was old, Abraham believed God. This pleased God. He spoke to Abraham again and said, "I will make my covenant (that is a very important promise) with you. I will give your descendants great lands. I will be their God and they will be my people." Again, Abraham trusted in God. Abraham lived a long life. He and his wife did have a son. Abraham was became known as the Father of Nations and the Father of our Faith.

The Ram - Isaac
(Genesis 22:1-19)

When Abraham was a very old man, God promised to make him the father of many nations. But he had no son. Even though his wife was too old to have children, God blessed her and she gave birth to a baby boy - Isaac. Isaac grew into a fine boy. Then, God tested Abraham. He sent Abraham to the top of a mountain, with Isaac, to make a sacrifice. Abraham asked "What am I to sacrifice?" God said "I will show you." As they climbed Isaac said "Where is the sacrifice?" Abraham said, "God will provide." At the top of the mountain, Abraham bound up Isaac and placed him on a pile of stones. Abraham thought God wanted him to give up his only son. Then an angel of the Lord stopped Abraham and showed him a ram stuck in a thicket. God was pleased with Abraham because he had obeyed. He had been willing to give up his only son for God.

The Ladder - Jacob

(Genesis 28:10-22)

Jacob was Isaac's son. One night he lay down in a field to rest for the night. He dreamed that he saw a ladder. The ladder went all the way from the earth up to the heavens. Angels were going up and down the ladder. Then he saw the Lord God standing next to him. God said to Jacob, "I am the God of Abraham and Isaac. I will bless you with many descendants. Your children will bless all the nations. I will be with you where ever you go." When Jacob woke up, he said, "God is in this place." He dedicated the place to God and called it Bethel which means "house of God." Then Jacob told God "I want you to be my God too."

The Coat - Joseph
(Genesis 37:1-45:28)

Jacob had 12 sons. Jacob loved Joseph more than the others. He gave Joseph a beautiful, many colored coat. His brothers were jealous. One day, Jacob sent Joseph into the fields to find his brothers. When his brothers saw him they said, "Oh, its Joseph. The favorite one." One brother said, "Let's throw him into a deep hole and leave him to die." But Reuben said, "No don't hurt him. We can sell him to some traders who will take him away to Egypt." So they did. At first, things were difficult in Egypt. Then Joseph had a dream about a coming famine. He told the King. The King made Joseph the Prime Minister (that's an important job). When the famine came, all the people were hungry but Joseph had stored up lots of food. The people came to him to get food. Even his brothers came. They did not know who he was. But he recognized them. He told them he loved them and that he had forgiven them.

The Basket - Moses
(Exodus 2:1-10)

Hundreds of years after Joseph and his brothers moved to Egypt, the Egyptians made the Israelites into slaves. The Egyptians decided that there were too many Israelites, so they made a law that all the baby boys must be taken away. A woman had a baby boy and she named him Moses. She saw how good he was, so she hid him for three months. When she couldn't keep him hidden any longer, she made a basket and set him in the reeds at the edge of the river. One day, the Egyptian King's daughter found the baby along the river bank. She took the baby up and decided to keep him as her own child. Moses' sister had been watching. She came to the Princess and asked if she needed someone to help her with the baby. When the Princess said yes, the girl ran to get her mother and bring her back. Moses grew up in the house of the King of Egypt.

The Tablets - Moses
(Exodus 20:1-17)

Moses led the Israelites out of slavery in Egypt. The people of God wandered in the desert for forty years. In the desert, God taught them about His law. Moses went up to the top of Mount Sinai. God wrote out Ten Commandments on stone tablets. He gave them to Moses to teach to the people.

1. I am the Lord your God. Worship no God but me.

2. Do not take the Lord's name in vain.

3. Keep Holy the Sabbath day of rest.

4. Honor your father and mother, *so that you may live a long life.*

5. Do not kill. (Respect life.)

6. Do not commit adultery. (Be pure.)

7. Do not steal. (Don't cheat.)

8. Don't make false accusations. (Don't lie)

9. Do not desire someone else's things. (Be grateful for what you have.)

10. Do not desire another person's spouse.

The Horn - Joshua
(Joshua 6:1-27)

Jericho was a great city. It had thick walls that went all the way around the city. God told Joshua to have the Israelites march around the city once a day for six days with the Arc of the Covenant in front of them. The Israelites thought this was strange. Some wondered how they could defeat a city by marching. Each day, they marched and the people of Jericho laughed at them. Then, on the seventh day, they marched around the city seven times blowing their horns. Joshua had done as God said. When they marched, on the seventh day, the Israelites blew their horns and all the men shouted. The walls of Jericho came tumbling down. They cheered. A miracle! God gave the city to the Israelites without a battle.

The Wheat - Ruth
(Ruth 1:1-4:22)

There was a widow named Ruth. Her mother-in-law, Naomi, said "Go back to your people." But Ruth was faithful. She went to Naomi's hometown with her. Because they were both widows, they were poor. Naomi was old. So, Ruth went into the wheat fields and picked the leftover wheat that the harvesters left behind. The man who owned the field was named Boaz. Boaz saw how kind Ruth was to Naomi and how well she cared for her mother-in-law. Boaz knew that Ruth was faithful. He asked Ruth to marry him. Ruth spoke with Naomi and decided that it would be good to marry Boaz. Boaz took care of Ruth and Naomi. Boaz and Ruth became the great-grandparents of King David.

The Tree - Jesse
(Isaiah 11:1, 10)

Jesse was King David's father. One day man came to Jesse's home. His name was Samuel. God had told him to go to Jesse's house and anoint the new King of Israel. Samuel asked to meet all of Jesse's sons. One by one, his sons came before Samuel but to each he said, "This is not the one." Finally, he asked, "Are these all your sons?" Jesse said, "No, my youngest is tending the sheep." He sent for David. When David appeared, Samuel anointed him King.

The prophet Isaiah had said that the Messiah (Jesus) would come from Jesse's family. "But a root shall sprout from the stump of Jesse, and from his roots a bud shall blossom." The prophet Isaiah said that the Spirit of the Lord would be on this ancestor of Jesse - the blossom from Jesse's roots. The Lord God would fill him with wisdom and understanding. He would be just and faithful. He would bring peace to the people and heal their wounds.

The Oil Lamp - Samuel
(1 Samuel 3:1-17)

When Samuel was a boy he lived with Eli the priest. One night, Eli was sleeping in his own room and Samuel was sleeping in the sanctuary. The Lord called out "Samuel, Samuel!" Samuel woke up. He ran to Eli and said "Here I am. You called." Eli said, "I didn't call you. Go back to bed." Samuel went back to bed. Then the Lord called out again, "Samuel, Samuel!" Samuel ran to Eli and said, "Here I am." Eli said, "Go back to bed, I didn't called you." Samuel went back to bed. Then the Lord called out a third time, "Samuel, Samuel!" He got up and went to Eli. "You called. Here I am." Then Eli realized that it was God calling Samuel. So he said, "Go back to bed and if you here your name called again say, 'Speak Lord, your servant is listening.'" Samuel went back to bed and this time when God called him, Samuel said, "Speak, Lord your servant is listening."

The Harp - David
(1 Samuel 16:1-23)

God sent the prophet Samuel to the house of a man named Jesse. God wanted Samuel to anoint one of Jesse's sons to be the next King. Jesse had his sons come before Samuel. Each time they came, Samuel thought "this must be the one." But God said, "No, not him." Samuel asked Jesse "Are these all your sons?" Jesse said, "No, my youngest is in the fields with the sheep." Samuel sent for him. When David came into the room God said "This is the one. Anoint him." So, David was anointed. Sometime later, King Saul began having tantrums. He couldn't calm down. He sent for someone to come and play the harp for him. David happened to be a very good harpist. David came and played the harp for Saul. When Saul had fits and tantrums, David would play. Then Saul would calm down and rest. David wrote many Psalms. He praised God by singing and dancing in worship.

The Crown - Solomon
(From 1 Kings 6:1-14)

When King David died his son, Solomon, became the new king. Shortly after Solomon became king he had a vision. The Lord asked Solomon "What gift would you like from me?" Solomon's answer was wisdom. God filled Solomon with great wisdom. He was a fair and just king. Solomon had a great temple built to honor God. It took seven years for Solomon to build the temple. It was filled with gold. The beams were made with cedar wood and the doors were made with olive wood. There were many beautiful carvings and statues. In the back of the temple was a room called the Holy of Holies. The Arc of the Covenant was placed in this room. The Arc was where Moses' stone tablets were kept. God's presence dwelled in the Holy of Holies.

The Stones - Elijah

(1 Kings 18:1-39)

Elijah was a prophet of the Most High God. His king was worshipping the false god Baal. The Lord God told Elijah to tell the king to stop. The king would not listen. Elijah said to the king and the prophets of Baal, "Let's see whose God is the true God." The prophets of Baal agreed. They built made an altar with stones and wood for a fire. They laid a bull on it and called out to Baal. But nothing happened. They tried many times, but nothing happened. Then Elijah made an altar with stones and wood for a fire. He soaked the wood with water. He laid a bull on top of the altar. Then Elijah called out to the Lord God. Then fire came from heaven and burned up the bull. It burned up the soaked wood. It burned up the rocks and dust and all the water that had spilled to the ground. All the people were amazed and cried out, "The Lord is God alone." The prophets of Baal were taken to jail and the king saw that he had been wrong to worship Baal.

The Walls – Nehemiah
(Nehemiah 1:1-7:73)

When Nebuchadnezzar was the king of Persia, he attacked Jerusalem and destroyed the walls of the city. The people who lived there were sent into exile. Many years later a man named Artaxerxes became king. At this time, there was an Israelite man named Nehemiah who lived in Persia. Some of his friends visited Jerusalem. When they returned they told him that the walls were sill in ruins. This made Nehemiah sad. He prayed to God. God told Nehemiah to go back to Jerusalem and fix the walls. Nehemiah returned to Jerusalem. He spoke to the people. They became excited to rebuild the walls. It wasn't an easy job. Some people didn't want the walls rebuilt. They made fun of the Israelites. They planned to keep the Israelites from rebuilding the walls. Nehemiah told the people to pray. God helped them. Miraculously, the walls were finished in only fifty-two days.

The Scroll - Isaiah
(Isaiah 40:1-11)

Isaiah was a prophet. He spoke about God's promise to send a Savior for the world. He spoke about hope in God's plan for redemption. One of Isaiah's prophecies said "A voice cries out, 'Proclaim a message!' 'What message shall I proclaim?' I asked. 'Proclaim that all mankind are like grass; they last no longer than wild flowers. Grass withers and flowers fade when the Lord sends the wind blowing over them. People are no more enduring than grass. Yes, grass withers and flowers fade, but the Word of our God endures forever. Jerusalem, go up on a high mountain and proclaim the Good News! Call out with a loud voice, Zion; announce the Good News! Speak out and do not be afraid. Tell the towns of Judah that their God is coming! The Sovereign Lord is coming to rule with power, bringing with him the people he rescued. He will take care of his flock like a shepherd; he will gather the lambs together and carry them in his arms; he will gently lead their mothers.'"

The Clay Pot - Jeremiah
(Jeremiah 18:1-12)

God said to Jeremiah, "Go to the potter's house. I have a message for you there." So, Jeremiah went. He watched the potter. The potter worked the clay on the wheel. If the piece wasn't perfect or if it didn't turn out how he wanted it to, the potter would just make it into something else. He could start all over if he wanted to. Then God gave Jeremiah the message. He said, "I am the potter, you are the clay. I can do with my people what I want. If I want to build up a nation, I will. If they become evil then I will not build them up. Tell my people to change their ways. Tell them to stop sinning. If they are obedient, I will work with them on my wheel and build them up."

Daniel and the Lions

Daniel worked for a king named Darius. He was a very good servant. King Darius decided to put Daniel in charge of his whole kingdom. Some of King Darius' other servants were jealous. They tricked King Darius into making a new law. This law said that no one could pray to any man or any god except Darius for thirty days. When Daniel heard that King Darius had agreed to the law, he was sad. But when he got home, he went upstairs and prayed to the Lord God anyway. The others had been waiting to trap Daniel. When they saw him pray to God, they arrested him and brought him to King Darius. King Darius had been tricked. The punishment for breaking this new law was to be thrown into a pit of lions. Daniel was not afraid to go to the lions. He put his trust in God. In the morning, King Darius sadly came back to the pit of lions. He thought Daniel would be dead. But Daniel was alive! The lions had not eaten him. King Darius said, "Truly, there is no god like Daniel's God."

The Fish - Jonah
(Jonah 1:1-4:11)

God told Jonah to go to Nineveh. He wanted Jonah to tell the people to change their ways. Jonah was afraid to go. He thought that he could runaway and hide from God. So, he got onto a boat going out to sea. A big storm came up. Everyone on the boat was frightened. Finally, Jonah stepped forward. He told the other sailors that it was his fault that God had sent the storm. The sailors prayed for God's mercy and threw Jonah overboard. A big fish came and swallowed Jonah up. Jonah spent three days and three nights in the belly of the fish. Then the fish spit him out onto the shore. Now, Jonah obeyed God. He went to Nineveh and told them to change their ways or God would destroy them. The whole city listened to Jonah, even the King. They put on sack cloths and ashes to show that they were sorry. God forgave the people of Nineveh. He did not destroy them or their city.

The Prayer Shawl - Zechariah and Elizabeth
(Luke 1:5-25)

There was a priest named Zechariah. He and his wife were very old and they had no children. One day, while he was serving in the temple, an angel appeared to him. Zechariah fell down in fear. But the angel said, "Do not be afraid. Your prayer has been heard and your wife will have a baby and you will name him John. And he will prepare the way for the Messiah." Zechariah could not believe what the angel had said. So the angel said that Zechariah would not be able to speak until the baby was born. And it happened that Elizabeth became pregnant and had a son. When he was born, the family asked what his name would be. Elizabeth looked to Zechariah and he spoke, for the first time since the vision, and said, "His name will be John."

The Shell - John the Baptist
(John 1:19-28)

When John grew up he went out into the desert. He lived there and ate locusts and honey. He wore a shirt made of camel's hair. The Word of God came to John "A voice cries out in the desert, prepare the way of the Lord." So, John began to go around preaching about the coming of the Messiah. One day, while John was preaching and baptizing people in the river, a man approached him. It was Jesus. John told Jesus "I should be baptized by you." But Jesus said "You baptize me. This way we will do all that God wants." So, John baptized him. Then the heavens opened and a dove came down. A voice said "This is my own dear Son with whom I am pleased." John kept preaching and baptizing. He was arrested by Herod. John would not stop preaching even in jail. At a great feast Herod's step daughter did a beautiful dance for him. Herod said she could have anything she wished. Her mother told her to ask for the head of John the Baptist. John was beheaded and his head was brought to the girl and her mother.

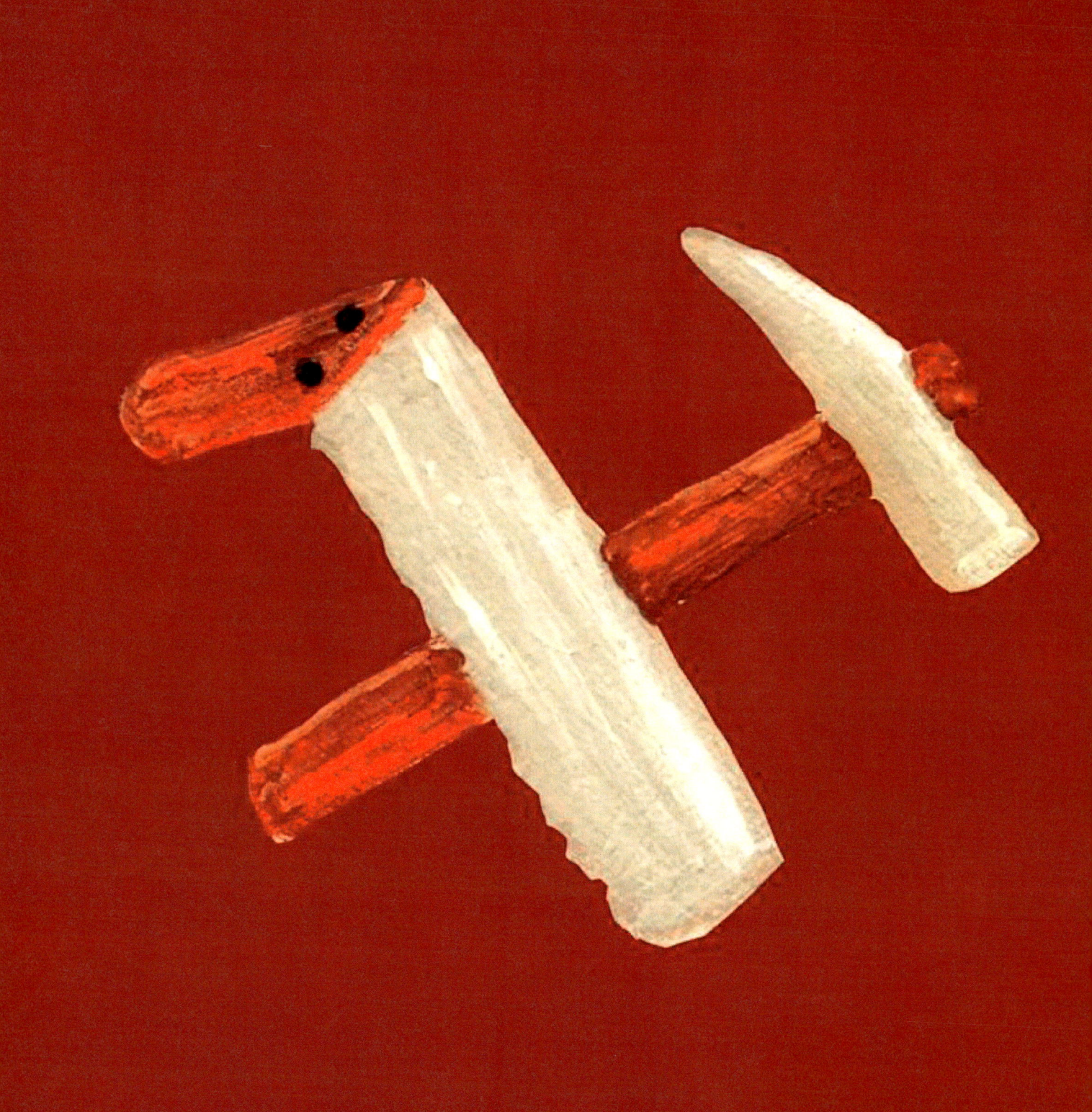

The Saw - Joseph
(Matthew 1:18-2:23)

Joseph was a carpenter. His family was descended from King David. He was a holy man who loved God. Joseph obeyed God and the laws God had given to his people. He became engaged to Mary, the Mother of our Lord. When Joseph found out Mary was going to have a baby, he was scared. They weren't even married yet. But God spoke to Joseph and told him to marry her. So, Joseph did. He listened to God and trusted him. Joseph was with Mary when Jesus was born. He took care of them and welcomed the shepherds and wise men who came to see the baby. He led Jesus and Mary to Egypt, when Herod was searching for the baby. When it was safe to return to Israel, Joseph led Mary and Jesus to Nazareth. He raised Jesus as his son. He taught him the skills of a carpenter. Jesus was obedient to Joseph.

The Angel - Gabriel
(Luke 1:26-2:52)

The angel Gabriel was sent to a young woman named Mary. He called to her, "Hail, full of Grace." This confused her. Then Gabriel said "Do not be afraid. You have found favor with God." And he told her that she was going to have a baby - a boy. Gabriel told Mary the baby's name would be Jesus. Mary did not understand how she could have a baby. She wasn't even married yet. Gabriel explained that God's Holy Spirit would come upon her and that the baby would be God's own Son. Gabriel sang praises about the baby, "He will be great and will be called the Son of the Most High. He will reign on David's throne and His Kingdom will have no end."

The Lily - Mary
(Luke 1:39-56)

After the angel Gabriel visited Mary, she traveled to see her cousin Elizabeth who was also expecting a baby. When Elizabeth saw Mary in the distance, the baby in her womb leaped. Elizabeth called out to Mary, "Blessed are you among women and blessed is the fruit of your womb." Mary replied saying, "My soul magnifies the Lord and my spirit rejoices in God my savior, for he has looked with favor on his lowly handmaid." Later, when the baby was born, Mary and Joseph named him Jesus. They took him to the temple to be dedicated to the Lord. A prophet named Simeon told Mary that one day a sword would pierce her heart. When Jesus grew up he was crucified on a cross. Mary was there when he died. She wept. She loved her son. It hurt to see him die like that. When Jesus rose again, Mary was one of the first people to receive the gift of His Holy Spirit. Mary now prays for us in heaven. She brings our needs to Jesus and pleads for us. She is not only his Mother but ours too.

The Star - Bethlehem
(Luke 2:1-14)

When Caesar Augustus was emperor, he decided to count all the people of his entire empire. All the people were to return to the town that there ancestors had come from. Joseph was from the family of King David and so he needed to return to Bethlehem. He took with him Mary who was still pregnant. When they arrived in Bethlehem, there were so many travelers, that Joseph could not find a place to spend the night. Finally, an innkeeper offered Joseph his stable as a warm dry place to rest. There the baby – the Lord of Heaven and Earth was born. They set him in a manger because they had no crib. All around the countryside a bright star emerged in the sky. It could be seen for hundreds of miles. There were shepherds in the fields and they looked at the star in wonder. Then an angel appeared to them and said, "Behold, I bring you Good News. For today, in Bethlehem is born a Savior, Christ the Lord! And this will be a sign for you; he will be wrapped in swaddling clothes, asleep in a manger."

The Manger -- Jesus
(Luke 2:15-20)

Jesus is the Son of the Living God. He was born in a humble manger in Bethlehem. A star rose in the east and the angels sang "Glory to God." Jesus grew up with his mother Mary and his foster-father Joseph. When he grew up he left home and began to preach the Word of God. He performed many miracles, healing the sick, forgiving sins. Some people thought he had come to take over as a great King. But, Jesus came to be King of our hearts, King of our lives. There were many who did not understand Jesus and were afraid of Him. They plotted together to have him killed. They arrested him, beat him and nailed him to a cross. There he died. Jesus died to save us from our sins. Three days later, Jesus rose from the dead! His tomb was empty. He greeted his apostles and said, "Peace be with you." He stayed with them for sometime and then he ascended into heaven to sit at the right hand of God. Then Jesus sent his Holy Spirit to help his apostles and disciples live a life that was holy. We can live that life too. Jesus loves us.